ESSENTIAL

BUY
HOME

SARAH PENNELLS
AND
MARC ROBINSON

LONDON, NEW YORK, MUNICH,
MELBOURNE, DELHI

Project Editor Richard Gilbert
Senior Art Editor Sarah Cowley

DTP Designer Rajen Shah
Production Controller Sarah Sherlock

Managing Editor Adèle Hayward
Managing Art Editor Marianne Markham
Category Publisher Stephanie Jackson

Produced for Dorling Kindersley by
PORTAL PUBLISHING
43 Stanley Street, Brighton
East Sussex BN2 0GP

Creative Director Caroline Marklew
Editorial Director Lorraine Turner

First published in Great Britain in 2003
by Dorling Kindersley Limited,
80 Strand, London WC2R 0RL

A Penguin company

2 4 6 8 10 9 7 5 3 1

Copyright © 2003
Dorling Kindersley Limited, London

Text copyright © 2003
Sarah Pennells
and Marc Robinson

A CIP catalogue record for this book is available
from the British Library

ISBN 0 7513 3728 5

Reproduced by Colourscan, Singapore
Printed in Hong Kong by Wing King Tong

See our complete catalogue at
www.dk.com

CONTENTS

SHOPPING FOR
A MORTGAGE

GETTING YOUR
MORTGAGE

BUYING YOUR
HOME

INTRODUCTION

Buying a home has the potential to be one of the most rewarding, yet most stressful experiences of your life. With its straightforward organization and simple explanations, Buying a Home is designed to help you feel more in control by making the process easy to understand and smoother to perform. Without committing hours of your valuable time, you will learn the terms, tasks, documentation, and the insights to help you buy the best home for you. There are many ways to make home ownership a reachable goal. This book will guide you step-by-step through the home-buying landscape so that the whole process of purchasing may be as satisfying as the experience of living in your new home.

MAKING PREPARATIONS

Understanding the basics of home buying and being prepared for all the steps involved will make your search easier, faster, and more enjoyable.

VIEWING THE MORTGAGE LANDSCAPE

There is a bewildering array of mortgage deals available nowadays and you will find it helpful to learn about sources of finance before you begin looking for a property.

BORROWING FUNDS

Very few buyers can afford a new home without taking on a mortgage. You will need to show that you are able to meet the repayments and that the property you are planning to buy is suitable. Gone are the days when you could only get a mortgage from your local building society or bank. Nowadays, as well as these traditional mortgage lenders, there are insurance companies and even supermarkets providing home loans, so the choice has become much wider.

CHOOSING BANKS

As well as traditional high street banks, an increasing number of financial institutions, such as insurance companies, have set up their own banking subsidiaries. Like many high street players, they offer loans and information over the internet, although with traditional banks you can often deal with your local branch if you prefer.

APPLYING TO BUILDING SOCIETIES

Unlike banks, building societies have no shareholders, so they do not need to pass on profits to them. Research has shown that building societies tend to offer more competitive rates overall, but that does not mean that every mortgage deal is a good one and they may not come up with the best deal for your particular circumstances.

GOING THROUGH SUBSIDIARIES

A number of mainstream lenders, whether banks, building societies, or insurance companies, have set up their own divisions to cater for specific sectors of the market. An increasing trend, for example, is to have a self-contained subsidiary that will deal with higher-risk borrowers (often called "non status" or "impaired credit"). It means that, even if one part of the lending organization has turned you down, another may be able to help.

USING MORTGAGE PACKAGERS

Some companies act as packagers, which means they market another lender's products under their own name. They deal with all the administration, for which they get a fee. Packagers' loans often have different rates and features from the lender's own-branded mortgages and they are normally available via brokers. You can find mortgages from packagers that cater for borrowers across the mortgage market.

IT'S A FACT

The number of home sales that took place in the United Kingdom over the last few years has been pretty steady at between 1.43 and 1.47 million a year.

RENTING OR BUYING?

Deciding whether to rent or buy may not be a straightforward decision, but there are some factors that will influence you.

COMPARING MONETARY ISSUES

Renting:

● Few or no maintenance costs.
● Smaller deposit. Normally you will need only one month's rent in advance and one month's rent as a deposit.
● You cannot lose money from falling home values.
● Moving expenses in and out.
● Can be seen as "lost" money – nothing to show for it at the end.
● Less security – your landlord may decide to sell.
● Rent can increase according to market conditions.

Owning:

● Monthly mortgage repayments tend to be lower than monthly rent payments.
● Property prices can rise, increasing your investment's value.
● Property can also fall in value.
● High upfront costs.
● Deposit of at least 5% of the purchase price usually required.
● Mortgage rates can be highly unpredictable.
● Moving expenses in and out.
● Ongoing responsibility for repairs and maintenance.

IT'S A FACT
The all-items retail price index (RPI), which measures how the cost of living changes, includes rental costs in its calculations.

> A home may be good inflationary protection because most homes rise in value during inflation.

CONSIDERING OTHER FACTORS

Renting:
- Easy to move out.
- No responsibility for structural repairs and upkeep.
- Time to assess an area before making a permanent decision to live there.
- Less stressful than buying a home.
- May have restrictions on noise, use, design, pets, children, and so on.

Owning:
- Usually more control over home design and improvements.
- Fewer restrictions on who occupies the home or how you use it.
- Satisfaction of owning your home.
- Moving typically requires more preparation and time.
- Continuous responsibilities for maintaining the building.
- If you do not like the area, it could be hard to move on in a hurry.

INVESTING IN PROPERTY

According to the Royal Institution of Chartered Surveyors, homes have risen in value by 8.4% a year on average. With a mortgage, that can make buying a home a very shrewd investment.

1. You buy a £200,000 home and put down £20,000 (10%).
2. The property appreciates by 5% a year for three years to £231,525.
3. Aside from other costs, you have earned a 157.6% return on your investment in three years. The reason for the impressive return is that, although your home cost £200,000, you invested only £20,000. The £31,525 increase in value on that £20,000 works out to be a 157.6% return.

On the other hand, that huge return may not give you as much profit as you think. There may be a considerable amount of other costs that would reduce your return. For example, you will have paid some additional costs, such as legal fees and stamp duty. You will also have paid surveyors' fees. In the end, most experts agree that people should buy a home first to be happy living in it, and second as an investment opportunity.

MOVING OFTEN?

First-time buyers tend to move after the shortest time, after five years on average, but according to the Council of Mortgage Lenders, the average length of time people remain in their home is 14.6 years.

WORKING OUT HOW MUCH YOU CAN AFFORD

*Y*our cash savings, monthly income, and credit record all factor into how much you can afford to spend on a home. This information is important to lenders as well as to you.

PURCHASE PRICE ▬

IT'S A FACT

The Council of Mortgage Lenders says that the amount people are borrowing to buy property is rising steadily, although the amount that first-time buyers are borrowing is growing by less than those already on the property ladder. Recent figures show that first-time buyers typically borrowed around £67,000, while those who already owned property borrowed £84,000 on average.

DEPOSIT ▬

The deposit is the percentage of the purchase price you pay in cash.

More cash, smaller loan. The more cash you pay, the smaller your loan will be. If you are a second-time buyer, you are likely to be able to pay a larger deposit. Anyone who can pay 25% or more could qualify for a much better mortgage deal.

Less cash, larger loan. If you are a first-time buyer you may only be able to come up with a 5% deposit, which is the minimum most lenders require. This will enable you to get a mortgage, but if you can come up with 10% it will widen your choice of loan.

FINDING THE DEPOSIT

Where will you get the cash? Here are some of the many possibilities:

- Cash in the bank or building society.
- Savings and investments you can afford to sell, but watch out for early surrender penalties and any tax implications.
- Valuables you would not mind selling (it is like exchanging them for a larger valuable, such as a home).
- Windfalls or bonuses from work.
- Gifts or loans from friends or relatives.

2 If you do not have a deposit, try to start saving now – setting up a standing order from your bank account may help.

MORTGAGE

There are different elements to your mortgage repayments, depending on the type you have:
Interest. You have to pay the lender interest on the loan every month.
Capital. With a repayment mortgage, part of your repayment goes towards repaying the capital (the amount you borrowed).
Investment. With interest-only loans, you may have an investment plan to pay off the capital.

CALCULATING AFFORDABILITY

How much can you afford every month?
Monthly income. Your salary and 50% of your past year's bonuses will be taken into account. Investment income is not usually accepted and neither is income from property unless you have a buy-to-let mortgage. Share dividends are taken into account if you have more than a 20% shareholding, when you are treated as self-employed.
Monthly debt. Subtract from your income the amount you pay in fixed debts, such as car loans, personal loans, and other regular payments. Do not include debts that will be cleared soon, but include variable payments such as credit card bills.

CONSIDERING OTHER COSTS

Many people do not consider (or prefer not to consider) all the associated costs of home buying. You will find information on all of these costs in this book. As an overview, you will probably pay:
- Solicitor's and surveyor's fees.
- Mortgage indemnity guarantee (MIG) – if your deposit is small. It protects the lender if you fail to repay. However, some lenders are now dispensing with this.
- Home insurance.
- Moving costs.
- Maintenance costs, and a service charge if you buy a leasehold flat.
- Utilities – they may cost more than they do in your current home.

TRYING BEFORE YOU BUY

If you are not sure whether you can afford all the costs involved, estimate their monthly total, and set that amount aside every month.

3 An emergency fund can be invaluable, particularly for first-time buyers.

MEETING LENDERS' CRITERIA FOR LOANS

*L*enders want you to take out a loan that is within your ability to repay. *They have varying formulas to make their calculations, but they adjust their criteria depending on the amount of your deposit and the reliability of your income. Lenders look at the profile of the home as well as your profile because both are important in assessing their risk.*

4 The amount you borrow and the term of the loan determine monthly repayments.

ASSESSING YOUR DISPOSABLE INCOME

Lenders consider how much your income can support. Your monthly housing expenses should be between 25% and 45% of your gross monthly income, depending on where you live.

CONSIDERING LONG-TERM DEBT

Generally lenders will take all your long-term debts into consideration. Any debt that will take at least one year to repay is considered to be a long-term debt. Some lenders will be more flexible than others when it comes to how much debt a borrower can have – it will depend on your credit score and the percentage of the property price you need to borrow.

BORROWING WHEN SELF-EMPLOYED

Borrowers will need to provide:
- Accounts for the last two years, or an accountant's certificate if self-employed for less than two years.
- Bank statements for at least the last three months.
- Rental or mortgage payment history for the last six months.

REVIEWING YOUR CREDIT HISTORY

Lenders are swayed by your credit history. Increasingly important is your *credit score*. This is a system of assessing how good a risk a potential borrower will be. The criteria used vary from lender to lender, but are not solely related to your debts. Borrowers with excellent credit will get the best choice of loans. Borrowers with lesser credit may not be denied altogether, but may have to approach a number of lenders and could be asked to pay a higher interest rate.

USING THE LOAN-TO-VALUE RATIO

Equity is important to lenders, too. Although they are not concerned about your profit, they do want to be repaid, earn a profit from interest, and avoid losses. So they look at the loan-to-value ratio (LTV). This is the difference between the loan amount and the home's market value. So if the lender gives you a loan of £75,000 on a £100,000 home, the loan-to-value ratio is 75%. The bigger the difference between the loan amount and the home's value, the smaller the loan-to-value ratio. The difference is called the *equity*. Lenders are rarely willing to finance loans of more than 100% LTV. Even so, these loans are extremely high risk and therefore more expensive.

FINDING FUNDS FOR A DEPOSIT

*S*ometimes, *the only difference between renting and being able to afford to buy a home is the cash you have available for a deposit. In today's market, home buying can be within reach even for people with little cash, although mortgage insurance can make it more costly.*

CALCULATING HOW MUCH YOU NEED

When property prices rise sharply for a number of years, many first-time buyers feel under pressure to "get on the housing ladder". They worry that they will never be able to afford their own home. If you are struggling to get a deposit and borrow as much as you need, there may be other options available to you, such as buying with friends or opting for a part-rent/part-buy scheme. However, you should be very careful about overstretching yourself. Interest rates have been very low for a few years, but they could rise again in the future – and sharply.

PROTECTING THE LENDER

Unless you can come up with a 25% deposit, you may be charged a mortgage indemnity guarantee (MIG) fee. Although the policy protects the lender in the event that you cannot keep up your mortgage payments, you have to pay for the policy. However, there is an increasing number of lenders that do not charge an MIG fee – even on loans of up to 90% – and some will let you borrow 95% without having to pay an MIG fee. Ask your mortgage broker.

GETTING HELP FROM THE FAMILY

Some first-time buyers borrow money from relatives – normally parents – to help them with their deposit, and many parents are keen to help their children. However, do not forget that, if it is a loan, you must be able to afford to repay it on top of your mortgage costs.

DEPOSIT	YOUR OPTIONS
0%	From time to time, lenders may let you borrow 100% of the purchase price. However, it is a riskier option. If you need to sell the property in the near future, or if property prices fall, you could owe more than the value of the mortgage (this is known as *negative equity*).
5%	Many housing experts believe that saving for a deposit is a good discipline that will make budgeting for the mortgage easier. If you have saved a 5% deposit, you will find it easier to get a mortgage than you will without one.
6–24%	A deposit of 6–24% will make a much wider range of mortgages available to you, although you may still be required to pay an MIG fee.
25% or more	Lenders believe that these buyers are most likely to repay their loan. Since they are lower risk, they are given better terms and do not have to pay an MIG fee.

UNDERSTANDING HOW MIG WORKS

An MIG policy does not directly protect you. It protects the lender in case a homeowner fails to make mortgage payments, a default occurs, and the home has to be repossessed. The homeowner will lose the home and all the money already put into it. The lender will be stuck trying to recoup the money it loaned. Mortgage indemnity guarantee protects lenders against financial costs if a homeowner defaults and the property is sold at a loss.

5 Avoid adding your MIG fee to your loan. You will pay interest on it for the whole term of the loan.

▼ BRIDGING THE GAP
Even if you do not have a large deposit, that will not necessarily prevent you from buying the house you want. MIG acts like a bridge to help fill the gap between you and your dream, but remember you will be charged for it and it can be expensive.

ARRANGING YOUR MORTGAGE IN ADVANCE

A greeing a mortgage ahead of finding your property, through an agreement or mortgage-in-principle certificate, is a useful service provided by most lenders. It gives you credibility with sellers. You are not obliged to take a mortgage from the lender who gives you this service.

PREARRANGING A LOAN

You normally have to fill in an application form to get a mortgage-in-principle certificate. You can do this either at the local branch of the lender or by post. You should provide details of:

- The amount of cash you plan to use as a deposit.
- Your gross monthly income.
- Your monthly debts.

Based on the information you have provided, the mortgage adviser will estimate how large a mortgage you would be able to have. It will not take details of your property into account.

6 Lenders will carry out a check of your credit file before deciding whether to offer you a mortgage in principle.

BENEFITING FROM A PREARRANGED LOAN

You benefit from a mortgage-in-principle offer in many ways:

- You may find out you can afford more than you thought.
- When you tell home sellers you have an agreement in principle, you gain instant credibility and have more leverage to bargain for a better price – the seller knows you have the mortgage and can afford the property.
- You can speed up the mortgage application process. The lender should only need to do another credit check to make sure your circumstances have not changed, and carry out a valuation of the property.
- You will discover in advance whether there are any problems with your credit, before you find your dream home. Once you are alerted to any problems, you will have a chance to put them right before you actually need a mortgage.
- You can decide whether or not the lender is the right one for you, which keeps you in control.

UNDERSTANDING HOW LENDERS BENEFIT

Mortgage-in-principle certificates help lenders benefit because:

- In a competitive mortgage marketplace, it will help them win customers who are under pressure to move quickly.
- It makes the process much easier and more efficient. Time is not wasted processing applications that would not be successful because of a credit or income problem.

Ms. Kristina Ambridge
1 Any Street
Anytown
WX12 3YZ

Dear Ms. Ambridge

Re: Mortgage-In-Principle Certificate

I am writing with regard to your qualifications for the purchase of a property up to the value of £70,000.

I can confirm that we have reviewed this matter at length and that you are qualified to purchase a property up to the aforesaid value. This calculation was made assuming a deposit of 5% is made on the new home. We have also reviewed your credit and received written confirmation of the necessary income.

7 An agreement in principle does not guarantee that you will get the loan.

UNDERSTANDING YOUR CREDIT FILE

T*he credit reference agencies hold information on almost all of us. Your credit file is a factual record of your borrowing and any debts you have; it does not make judgments about whether or not you should be allowed a loan.*

OBTAINING YOUR CREDIT FILE

You have a legal right to see the information that is stored on your credit file. You can either apply in writing, enclosing a cheque or postal order for the small fee involved, or you can telephone and pay with a debit or credit card. Contact all three credit reference agencies so that you have all the information stored about you. They will be able to give you details of the current fee.

DEALING WITH THE DATA ON YOUR FILE

When you receive a copy of your credit file, the first thing you should do is check that the information is correct. If there are any errors or negative items such as unpaid debts, you should get them sorted out as soon as possible or they may affect your ability to obtain a mortgage. You can deal with a negative item as follows:

- Pay off any amounts you owe, then ask the creditor to update your credit file accordingly.
- Wait for the negative item to be removed automatically (usually after six years).
- Send in a written explanation of the debt and ask the agency to add it to your file. The item will not be removed, but future creditors will take your explanation into consideration.

8

Around three-quarters of a million people request copies of their credit files each year.

ACTING ON A REFUSAL

A lender does not have to tell you why you were refused credit, but it must inform you if credit reference information played a part in that decision and, if so, which agency supplied the information. Contact the agency first. If you are still in doubt or experiencing problems after contacting the agency, you can contact a consumer organization such as the Citizen's Advice Bureau, which you can find in your local telephone book, or log on to www.nacab.org.uk. You can also contact the Consumer Credit Counselling Service by telephoning 0800 138 1111, or log on to www.cccs.co.uk.

CONTACTING CREDIT REFERENCE AGENCIES

Here are the three credit reference agencies and their contact details:

Equifax
Credit File Advice Centre
PO Box 3001
Glasgow G81 2DT
Tel: 0870 514 3700
Website: www.equifax.co.uk

Experian Limited
Consumer Help Service
PO Box 8000
Nottingham NG1 5GX
Tel: 0870 241 6212
Website: www.uk.experian.com

Callcredit PLC
Consumer Services Team
PO Box 491
Leeds LS1 5XX
Tel: 0870 060 1414
Website: www.callcredit.plc.uk

IDENTIFYING COMMON PROBLEMS

Credit reference agencies say they have stringent checks in place to make sure information is accurate, but the only way to be sure is to order your file and check that:

- Credit information relates only to you and not to anyone else with the same address and surname.
- Negative data has been removed or amended once debts are paid.

Looking for a Home

You can use a variety of tactics to find your home.
Choices abound and the options can seem confusing, especially
if you are a first-time buyer. Here is a guide.

Getting Started

Most buyers still use an estate agent to help them find the right
property. You do not have to pay them a fee – sellers pay them.
However, there are many other sources you can use.

Using the Internet

The internet is becoming increasingly
important as a tool for prospective home
buyers. However, most people are still using
it in addition to an estate agent, not instead
of one. There are some private sale sites
on the internet, but generally many
property sites simply refer you to
the relevant estate agent for
further details.

SEARCHING THE INTERNET

Property search websites. These are useful if you want to check out the prices in an area and see what is available on the market, or how far your money will go.

Estate agents' websites. These sites carry details of properties that are available. They have become increasingly sophisticated: most carry a photograph of the property and some websites have "virtual" property tours.

Private sale websites. Private owners who do not want to involve an estate agent post details of their property, plus how to get in touch.

GETTING UP-TO-DATE INFORMATION

Local newspapers are often a useful source of property advertisements. Many papers produce a regular property supplement as well. The main problem is that the advertisements are supplied days, and sometimes over a week, in advance, so a property could be sold before you get a chance to follow it up. However, they should give you a good feel for the state of the market.

9 Private sale information is not covered by the same rules and regulations as that given by estate agents.

LOGGING ON TO PROPERTY WEBSITES

If you are trying to find property websites, the simplest way to access them is to type something like "houses for sale" into a search engine. This will give you a selection of property sites. You can then refine your search according to what you are seeking. Type in the area you are considering, the type of property (such as maisonette, flat, house), how many bedrooms, and price range. Some sites are better than others at letting you refine your criteria in a meaningful way. Here are a few sites to consider:

● www.fish4homes.co.uk
● www.assertahome.co.uk
● www.propertyfinder.co.uk
● www.hol365.com

If you want more detailed information, you will be referred to the estate agent dealing with the sale. Private sale listings can be found on a number of sites, including:

● www.houseweb.co.uk
● www.mondial-property.co.uk
● www.propertybroker.com
● www.privatehousesforsale.com

USING AN ESTATE AGENT

K nowing how to get the estate agent on your side can make the whole buying process much easier.

COMMUNICATING WITH YOUR AGENT

Before you begin the search for your dream home, make sure you and your estate agent have the same ideas.

Stay in touch. Find out the best times to phone in for updates on what is coming to the market. Make sure the agent has all your contact numbers. If you can only view property at certain times, say so.

Set your priorities. Save time by not following up particulars that do not meet your criteria. Clearly set your priorities with your agent.

Be opinionated. Be truthful about what you like and do not like about a property's condition, floor plan, and other specifications so your agent can find homes that better suit your preferences.

Take advantage of your agent's knowledge. Ask your agent to let you know about properties that are about to be listed. Be prepared to drive by or visit a property at short notice.

FINDING AN AGENT

Try the internet (type "estate agent" into a search engine), the local paper, or a local telephone directory for names and contact details of estate agents. If you prefer, go to the local high street and look in estate agents' windows. Alternatively, note the agents' names that appear on "For Sale" boards in your chosen area.

REGULATING ESTATE AGENTS

What estate agents say about a property is covered by law. The Property Misdescriptions Act 1991 says they must not knowingly misdescribe the property or give false or misleading information.

GETTING ESTATE AGENTS ON YOUR SIDE

In a competitive property market, it is especially important that the agent thinks of you when a new property comes on the market. Get to the top of the list by:

- Seeing estate agents face to face. Either arrange to meet them at their offices at a time that is convenient (late in the afternoon is normally a good idea, when they have returned from lunchtime viewings), or have a chat with them sometime during the first viewing.
- Ensuring that the agent knows exactly what you want.
- Arriving on time for viewings, and never cancelling at the last minute.
- Finding out from the agents whether what you are looking for is impossible, a rarity, or in their mainstream market.
- Showing the agents that you are an organized and serious buyer. It always helps if you can demonstrate that you have already got your mortgage agreed in principle, subject to the right property being found.

THINGS TO KNOW

- As you progress in your search for your new home, you will get a much clearer idea of which estate agents you are finding the most helpful. If an agent is doing a good job, let him or her know. Positive feedback is always welcome. However, as with any profession, the standard of service among estate agents can vary. Therefore if you have any complaints, do not be afraid to tell the agent, but make sure you keep to the issues. Do not blame the agent if you are not successful in your bid to buy a property you liked: agents can make recommendations to sellers about whether an offer represents good value, but ultimately the decision about who is going to be the successful buyer is not theirs.
- If an agent is a member of the National Association of Estate Agents (NAEA), it should display the NAEA logo on its premises or stationery and there is a code of conduct and a complaints procedure if you are unhappy. Alternatively, if the estate agent is a member of the Ombudsman for Estate Agents Scheme (around a third of estate agents are members), the Ombudsman may investigate your complaint.

IT'S A FACT

Do not forget that, no matter how helpful the estate agent is being, it is the seller who will be paying the agent's fee.

UNDERTAKING RESEARCH

Searching for a home can be a stressful activity. It is important that you start your search with clear priorities about what you want, both in a home and a neighbourhood, and then do some careful research.

MAKING A WISH LIST

Think about what features you must have, would like to have, and do not need in your home. Be specific. For example, do you really need an attached garage, or do you just think it would be nice to have one? Would off-street parking do?

FINDING A BARGAIN

You may think the only way you will be able to afford a property is to buy something run down and do it up yourself. This could be a good idea, but it could also go wrong. Get advice from the experts before you take the plunge:

- Look for bargain homes that need only minor repairs.
- Make sure the basic layout of the property is sound.
- Always have the property inspected by a surveyor (and ideally a builder) before buying.
- Get an estimate of repair costs.
- Do not spend money on improvements that will not actually add value.

STUDYING THE HOUSING MARKET

One of the characteristics of the housing market is that it is becoming increasingly localized. Prices can very widely – not just from one part of a town or city to another, but from street to street. Local factors that help determine the price include:

Transport links. A property that has good transport links can be more expensive than one that does not.

Schools. Family homes that are in the catchment area of a school that performs well often sell quickly, and at a premium.

Jobs. If a new business is moving to an area, or it is undergoing major expansion, prices can rise as some workers relocate.

Restaurants/shops. The opening of a few restaurants, pubs, or shops can add to the price of an area.

Roadworks/building projects. If they are likely to be disruptive, they can have a negative effect on property prices.

IT'S A FACT

The stamp duty threshold has been increased in around 2,000 designated deprived areas. As a result, more property purchases in deprived areas in the UK will be free from stamp duty.

RESEARCHING NEIGHBOURHOODS

If you are buying a home locally, drive through your chosen neighbourhoods. Look in estate agents' windows to get a feel for prices. Whether you are buying locally or further afield, check the internet for information on specific areas, such as schools, crime statistics, local amenities, transport links, and any other information that you feel would be useful to know.

> **10** Keep in mind that selecting the right home almost always requires some compromise in what you would like to have.

ASSESSING RISKS

Flooding and contaminated land risks have become much more important issues for prospective homeowners over the last few years. In some areas, you could have problems reselling and even getting insurance for a home that is at risk. The Environment Agency (log on to www.environment-agency.gov.uk) has information on environmental risks. Another useful site (log on to www.homecheck.co.uk) gives free information on environmental risks – simply type in your postcode.

▼ **TARGETING AREAS**
Focusing your search on two or three neighbourhoods will help you master your understanding of those areas and keep you from becoming overwhelmed and confused.

UNDERSTANDING LEASEHOLD PROPERTIES

Usually houses are freehold and, in England and Wales, flats are leasehold, but there are exceptions. Basically, freehold means that you own the property outright, whereas leasehold means that you have restricted rights.

DEFINING LEASEHOLD

When you buy a leasehold flat (or occasionally a leasehold house), you do not actually own the property. What you are purchasing instead is the right to live there for a number of years (the time remaining on the *lease*). The landlord, also known as the *freeholder*, owns the property – it can be an individual or a company, or it can even be the flat owners (called *leaseholders* or *lessees*) who live there. As a leaseholder, you have fewer rights over your flat than ordinary homeowners (who buy freehold property), but you still have responsibilities towards the upkeep.

CALCULATING LEASEHOLD COSTS

You normally have to pay a service charge (which generally includes buildings insurance), plus the cost of repairs and maintenance. You will also have to pay ground rent to the landlord, which can be anything from around £50 to £300 or more a year. Leasehold blocks are normally managed on a day-to-day basis by managing agents, who are hired by the landlord but paid for by the lessees. It is possible for the lessees to manage their own blocks, or to buy out the landlord's interests entirely. However, you are still responsible for maintaining the building between you. Managing agents normally charge an annual fee for overseeing maintenance of the flats.

You should study your lease – it is a legal agreement between you and your landlord.

EXTENDING A LEASE

Leaseholders have the right to extend the length of their lease, as long as they pass some qualification criteria, and so some mortgage lenders have started to become more relaxed about how many years are left unexpired when you buy. Some lenders are more flexible than others, however, so try to ensure that your lease has a minimum of 50 years remaining after the mortgage has been paid off. A longer lease will normally be cheaper to extend than a shorter one, so if you are considering extending the lease once you have bought the property, it is worth bearing in mind.

USING A SINKING FUND

Find out if the property has a sinking fund (money put by) to cover emergencies. It is the best way to help cushion the blow of repairs and any ongoing maintenance.

PURCHASING A LEASEHOLD HOUSE

In some areas, typically the north of England, there is a number of estates made up of leasehold houses. Here you do not pay a service charge for ongoing upkeep of the property, but you do have to pay the landlord ground rent. It is often only a few pounds a year, but the landlord still has the power to add on any administrative and legal costs if you do not pay on time.

THINGS TO KNOW

- Leaseholders now have more rights, thanks to recent legislation. They can challenge repair bills that they think are unreasonable, or take over the management of the block. Buying a leasehold flat does not mean you will be taking on problems, but there is more potential for things to go wrong.
- If managing agents are involved, find out whether they are members of ARMA (the Association of Residential Managing Agents). It has a code of conduct and a complaints procedure.
- If you are considering a leasehold property, ask your solicitor to check the lease to make sure there are no onerous clauses. Also ask the seller and other lessees if they have a good relationship with the landlord.

USING A CHECKLIST

B y the time you have seen several properties, you will probably struggle to remember the good and bad points of each. It is worth taking a checklist to use as a reminder later on.

THE PROPERTY – OVERALL

Total rooms:

Bedrooms _____

Bathrooms _____

Kitchen:			
Size	good _____	average _____	poor _____
Fittings	good _____	average _____	poor _____
Living rooms:			
Size/shape	good _____	average _____	poor _____
Original features	good _____	average _____	poor _____
Aspect	good _____	average _____	poor _____
Size/shape of bedrooms	good _____	average _____	poor _____
Storage space	good _____	average _____	poor _____
Parking availability	good _____	average _____	poor _____
Level of property maintenance	good _____	average _____	poor _____

THE LOCATION

Journey to work	easy _____	average _____	difficult _____
Journey to schools	easy _____	average _____	difficult _____
Transport links	good _____	average _____	poor _____
Schools	good _____	average _____	poor _____
Shops	close _____	average _____	far _____
Doctor's surgery/hospital	close _____	average _____	far _____
Pubs/wine bars/restaurants	close _____	average _____	far _____
Bank/post office	close _____	average _____	far _____
Sports/health club	close _____	average _____	far _____
Parks/open spaces	close _____	average _____	far _____
Place of worship	close _____	average _____	far _____
Connection of gas/mains drainage	good _____	possible _____	difficult _____

GARDEN
___ Level and well-drained ground
___ Smooth and not-too-steep driveway
___ Gardens and lawns well established

FOUNDATION
___ No decay or mildew in basement
___ No rotting wood
___ No big cracks in concrete

STRUCTURE
___ No major cracks or sags in the walls
___ Floors are level
___ Roof is in good condition
___ No water stains on ceilings or walls
___ Rafters do not sag
___ No damage to visible joints and beams
___ Attic ceiling does not allow light to shine through
___ Chimneys are in good working order

EXTERIOR
___ Doors are not rotten; open and shut easily
___ Windows are weatherproof and not rotten
___ Paint is not peeling
___ Adequate gutters and drain pipes

12 Note practical details such as room sizes, availability of parking, and overall condition of the property.

INTERIOR
___ Property has been well maintained
___ Major appliances, including central heating boiler and water heater, are in good condition
___ Floors do not sag or creak
___ Carpets are in good condition
___ Electrical wiring has not deteriorated
___ Adequate ventilation
___ Good security
___ Doors close properly
___ Underlying problems are not masked by wallcoverings or damp-proof paint
___ Water pressure is good
___ Waste water drains quickly
___ Plumbing does not make much noise
___ No plumbing leaks around joints
___ Toilets operate well

COMPARING TYPES OF HOMES

PROPERTY TYPE	PROS	CONS
House	More ownership	More responsibility
Flat/apartment	You can share the cost of maintenance	You will have to pay ground rent and service charges
New home	Fewer maintenance costs	Fewer choices in property style and neighbourhood
Older home	Property often has more character	Can have higher repair and maintenance costs

MAKING YOUR CHOICE

*B*efore you make an offer on a property,
be sure you know all the pros and cons,
including market conditions, all your options,
and the price of comparable properties.

ASSESSING THE PROPERTY

Before you make an offer, review your
wish list and checklist, and the
property particulars, and weigh all the
factors carefully. Your purchase decision
and your offer depend partly on:

- Your priorities ranked in order of
  importance so you can weigh up
  which homes are the best match for
  the features you want.
- Comparable homes and how the
  homes that interest you compare to
  other homes in the area. Make sure
  you see them all in similar conditions.
  Go back at various times – weekends
  or in the evening, as well as during
  working hours. Even if you do not
  view the property each time, you can
  get a feel for the neighbourhood.
- Market conditions and whether the
  homes on your list are in a buyer's,
  seller's, or stable market. Remember
  that houses in a seller's market may
  command higher prices.
- The pros and cons of each home.
  Review the notes you took while
  visiting each home and look for
  qualities that match your priorities.
  Some trade-offs will be unavoidable.

13 Taking notes and
even photographs of
each home of
interest will help you
remember the details
and make you more
certain about your
final decision.

MAKING COMPROMISES

You are unlikely to find everything that is on your wish list in one property. In a rising market, when there is a shortage of property, it could be even more of a challenge. Make a list of qualities that you would like in your new home and another list of features that are really important to you. If the properties you have seen so far do not meet your requirements, you have two options:

● Compromise – decide how important the "missing" features really are. For example, could you live without a garden, or could you cope with a smaller bedroom or a longer walk to the bus stop/railway station?

● Think laterally – is there a way around your problem? For example, could you build on or convert an existing room into a different space? Could you knock through two small rooms to make one larger room, or add an en suite bathroom? Is there room to build a garage, or could you rent one nearby?

WEIGHING UP THE MARKET

Understanding market conditions makes you a better buyer. In a seller's market, housing demand is high and supply is low so buyers often have to pay full price or more for their homes. In a buyer's market, housing demand is low and supply is high so buyers are able to negotiate.

MAKING A DECISION

Weighing all the facts will clarify what you are willing or not willing to accept while you are negotiating with the seller. Make sure you are clear on:

● What you must have, what you would like to have, and what would be nice to have but is not worth the extra cost.

● What your overall pricing parameters are, such as the highest and lowest price you will offer based on the realities of the marketplace and how badly you want the property.

14 According to some sources, the average buyer looks at ten homes before buying.

MAKING AN OFFER

Once you find a property you like, the process can become more stressful. Unless the market is very quiet, you will have to move quickly. The more preparation you do in advance, the better.

1 SUBMITTING THE OFFER

When you put in an offer, how it will be treated depends on where the property is in the UK. For example, in England, Wales, and Northern Ireland, an offer is treated as an indication of intent, but is not legally binding. In Scotland, the offer is treated more formally, and is not normally made until a survey and mortgage have been arranged. However, whatever your circumstances, you should not make an offer just to buy yourself extra time.

2 NEGOTIATING THE PRICE

You do not want to pay more than is necessary, but do not haggle over a few hundred pounds just for the sake of it. Take advice from the estate agent, if you wish, but remember that the agent is employed by the seller to get the best price. If a property has been on the market for some time, the agent will probably have advised the seller to be prepared to negotiate.

3 RAISING THE OFFER

The seller is quite likely to reject your first offer, simply because many people see this as an "opening bid". However, it does not mean you will end up paying a lot more. Raise your offer in increments, if necessary, but try not to go over your original budget. It does not matter how much you offer – if you cannot get a loan you cannot buy the property.

KNOWING WHAT TO DO WHEN YOUR OFFER IS ACCEPTED

Even when your offer has been accepted, there could still be quite a long way to go. You may have your own property to sell and a mortgage to arrange. Ask the sellers or their estate agent if the property will be taken off the market, or if they will continue showing round potential buyers until contracts have been exchanged. Many estate agents advise sellers to continue showing round potential buyers if they believe the property could achieve a higher price, which means that another buyer could step in later with a higher offer.

UNDERSTANDING GAZUMPING

Gazumping, when someone else comes in with a better offer, is what every buyer dreads. It only happens in a minority of cases, but it can leave you financially worse off if you have started incurring fees.

4 WORKING WITH THE AGENT

Many buyers get frustrated when they lose their dream home and blame the estate agent. In some cases it may be justified, but remember that the estate agent is often just the messenger and not the one making the decision. Sellers sometimes get overambitious about how much they can make from the sale of their property. The estate agent is obliged to pass on all offers, but the seller has freedom over which one to accept. If you are up against a cash buyer and you need a mortgage, or the other buyer can complete the deal more quickly than you, you are unlikely to be at the top of the list. Try to get the agent on your side: sellers are often influenced by what the agents say.

5 ACTING QUICKLY

Your offer is dependent on contracts being exchanged as soon as possible. Do not waste time once your offer has been accepted – act quickly because any protracted delay will increase the chances of another buyer stepping in.

AGREEMENT FOR SALE AND PURCHASE	
Agreement Date:	
Property:	Flat 1, 1 High Building, Anytown WX12 3YZ
Seller:	RAJNEESH PATEL of Flat 1, 1 High Building, Anytown WX12 3YZ
Buyer:	JANE SMITH and JOHN SMITH both of 12a High Street, Anytown WX11 2QZ
Burdens on the Property:	All matters contained or referred to in the Property and Charges Registers save for financial charges
Title Guarantee:	The Property is sold with full title guarantee
Completion Date:	
Contract Rate:	The Law Society Rate
Root of Title/ Title Number:	
Purchase Price:	£75,000
Deposit:	£3,750

▲ REVIEWING THE PURCHASE CONTRACT

Your offer will not become legally binding until contracts have been exchanged between you and the seller. Dates are often left blank in the contract until the solicitors are ready to exchange. The contract should cover every aspect of the agreement, such as:

- *Legal description of the property.*
- *Sale price, payment terms, and amount of the deposit.*
- *Who gets the deposit if the deal is not completed (this will be shown in the standard conditions annexed to the contract).*
- *The seller's promise to provide clear title to the property.*
- *Completion date.*
- *Details of any burdens on the property.*
- *Description and price of any chattels that are to be added to the purchase.*
- *Whether the property is sold with limited or full title guarantee depending on the seller's capacity to sell.*

SHOPPING FOR A MORTGAGE

The choice of mortgages can be bewildering. A mortgage is a long-term contract, so it is important to understand what you are taking on and to do some research to get the best deal.

UNDERSTANDING LOAN DEALS

*V*ery few people sign up for a standard variable rate mortgage, (a loan where the interest rate fluctuates). There are many more competitive deals on offer, which will help you with budgeting.

BEST BUYS						
Lender & Contact	Initial Rate	Type	Period	LTV	Fee	Redemption Penalty
Short/Medium Term						
First Building Society	3.59%	2.25% discount	2 years	75%	£295	2 years
Second Building Society	3.84%	1.75% discount	3 years	75%	£295	3 years
Universal Bank	4.79%	Fixed	2 years	95%	£295	2 years
Long Term						
Global Bank	4.09%	2.15% discount	5 years	75%	None	5 years
Worldwide Bank	5.49%	Fixed	5 years	80%	£295	5 years
Third Building Society	5.45%	Capped at 5.99%	5 years	95%	£300	5 years
Flexible Mortgages						
Universal Bank	2.85%	2.00% discount	6 months	90%	None	None
First Building Society	2.99%	2.22% discount	6 months	75%	None	3 years
Global Bank	4.99%	Fixed	1 year	75%	£199	None

◀ **SHOPPING AROUND**
Many newspapers carry tables like this in their personal finance supplements. Although the table may show outdated information, since mortgage offers can be withdrawn at short notice, it will give you a sense of the market. The internet also carries mortgage rate information.

15 An independent financial adviser will shop around for you.

Keep your cash . . .
You can avoid upfront fees and other charges that you would normally pay to the lender, but expect to pay more in the longer term, probably through a higher rate and higher monthly repayments.

NO FEES

6.56%	7.07%
FIXED	APR

LOW RATES
4.75%   8.20% APR

. . . or make low monthly repayments.
Pay more fees up front and you can lower your repayments. If the APR is much higher than the interest rate, this may indicate that the lender is charging high upfront fees.

Stretch repayments . . .
Spread them over the longest possible time. You will repay the loan slowly, and pay much more interest overall, but each repayment will be as low as possible.

25 Year Term

7.5% 7.85% APR

15 Year Term

7.125% 7.5% APR

. . . or repay quickly.
You will have higher monthly repayments, but more of each payment will go towards repaying your loan. That means you will be building equity faster.

Take a chance . . .
Go for the lowest possible rate now and hope that rates do not rise substantially after the discount period ends.

. . . or play it safe.
Get a fixed rate you know you can afford and you will be able to plan your future finances around it.

1 year discount	3 year discount
4.50% 7.41% APR	5.87% 8.11% APR

10 year fixed	5 year fixed
7.31% 7.69% APR	6.05% 7.91% APR

NON-STATUS LOANS

Not so much paperwork or so many questions.
Consider this option if you cannot prove you have enough income, or have had debt problems in the past, but expect to pay for the privilege in upfront cash or a higher rate of interest.

Term of the loan
The longer you take to repay the loan, the smaller each repayment will be, but the loan will cost you more because you will owe more in interest. The less time you take to repay the loan, the higher each repayment will be, but you will build your equity quicker and pay less interest.

Long-Term Loans

30 year term

6.2%   6.85 APR

Interest rate
The interest rate set by the lender determines the amount of interest you will pay at each instalment.

Annual percentage rate (APR)
The APR is a more accurate expression of your yearly cost of borrowing than just the interest rate. It takes into account the interest and other costs such as the credit check, mortgage insurance, and broker's fees. These costs are then spread over the life of the loan.

GETTING LOAN ADVICE

Now that you have found your dream home and you know more about your mortgage options, you can start shopping for your loan.

APPROACHING LENDERS

Some people choose a loan by looking at a number of high street banks and building societies, and finding out what kind of mortgage deals they have. You do not have to go from branch to branch (although you can if you prefer), because most either have a telephone number that you can use to request information, or they display the information on their websites. Banks and building societies are limited in the loans they can offer you – you will not get a choice from across the market, which may mean you lose out on the best deals.

Shopping around. Not all lenders charge the same variable rate, and one lender may have a much better rate for you at that time. In addition, some are more flexible than others when it comes to lending criteria. Just because you may be turned down by one lender does not mean you will be turned down by the rest.

PLAYING BY THE RULES

Estate agents are not supposed to put pressure on buyers to use their own mortgage brokers, or imply that, unless buyers use the agent's broker, they will not be shown properties or their offer will have less chance of being accepted.

USING A BROKER

There are many different kinds of mortgage brokers, but the ones you are most likely to come across are either attached to an estate agent or operating separately (often as part of a larger independent financial advice practice). The status of the mortgage broker can be difficult to understand, but it is worth checking because it could affect the choice of products you are offered. A number of brokers are independent when it comes to arranging the loan (that is to say, they can select the mortgage from a number of lenders), but they may be restricted about whose investment polices (such as endowments or ISAs) they sell. Ask the broker to explain if you are unclear about his or her situation.

Choosing a broker. Personal recommendation is the best way to find a financial adviser, but if you cannot use that route, speak to several of them either face to face or over the telephone before you make your decision. Is the adviser listening to what you want or being pushy? Ask how he or she charges: many brokers charge either an arrangement fee or a commission on any products you buy, while others do not charge the borrower at all, but take a fee directly from the lender.

CHECKING COMMISSION RATES

Lenders often pay a fee to a financial adviser, known as an *introducer's fee*, when the purchase of a property is completed. Under the Mortgage Code issued by the Council of Mortgage Lenders, your financial adviser should provide you with details of this fee on request. Alternatively, you can request this information directly from the lender.

CHECKING THE INTERNET

There is a huge amount of information on the internet, which can be useful for your preliminary research. However, the standard of websites does vary. One problem with some of them is that you may appear to pass the lending criteria on-line, but fail when you actually make an application.

Selecting a Mortgage Rate to Suit You

There are many types of mortgage rate, and even if you are getting professional advice, it helps if you understand what they involve.

Choosing Between Variable or Fixed

Standard variable rate (SVR). This is the normal rate charged by the lender when no other discounts or special deals apply. It fluctuates according to market conditions, and is the rate that borrowers may have to revert to for a limited time once their preferential mortgage deal has come to an end.

Fixed rate. Unlike an SVR, where the rate fluctuates in line with base interest rates (set by the Bank of England), this rate is fixed at the outset for a defined period of time. The lender buys the money in advance from the commercial money markets, so fixed rates tend to have early redemption penalties. They are more expensive when general interest rates are expected to rise, and cheaper when they are about to fall.

16 Fixed rates are invaluable for first-time buyers on a tight budget who want to be sure that their repayments will not rise.

Using Discount or Capped Rates

Discount rate. With this deal, the rate you pay rises and falls in line with base interest rates, but it is at a lower level (discount) to the standard variable rate. Generally, the bigger the discount, the shorter the time it will apply. Discounts often have lower rates than comparable fixed rates, but if your budget is tight and you will struggle to afford your mortgage if rates were to rise sharply, you should opt for the certainty of a fixed rate.

Capped rate. With a capped rate, the mortgage rate may fall, but it can only rise to a predetermined upper limit. It means you should get the best of both worlds – a cheaper rate when base interest rates are low, and a maximum above which your mortgage rate will never rise.

Setting Rates

The Bank of England sets interest rates as a way of controlling inflation. Lenders alter their own interest rates (apart from fixed rates) to reflect what the Bank of England has done.

OPTING FOR A TRACKER RATE

Tracker rate. Like the standard variable rate, a tracker rises and falls in line with base interest rates. However, unlike other variable rates, a tracker exactly mirrors changes made by the Bank of England. For example, if the Bank has reduced interest rates by 0.25%, your tracker will immediately fall by the same amount. A tracker rate is normally expressed as an amount above the Bank base rate, for example 0.75% above base rate. This amount can vary. It is important to check how long the tracker lasts, because some mortgages are lifelong trackers, while others last for only a few years.

EXPLORING OTHER MORTGAGE DEALS

Cashback. With this deal, when you take out a mortgage, you receive a cash sum, which can be from several hundred to several thousand pounds, and usually depends on the size of the loan. Your cashback may be combined with another preferential rate or with the standard variable rate. A cashback can help first-time buyers furnish their home, but it may not be the most competitive deal over the longer term.

Combination of rates. You do not have to limit yourself to just one rate. Many lenders will let you split your loan in two and have half on a fixed rate and half on a variable rate. Others will let you be even more creative and divide your loan into several tranches, with short- and longer-term fixed rates, for example.

THINGS TO KNOW

You should not simply look at the headline rate when choosing a mortgage. You should also consider other factors, including the following:

● Whether the lender charges an MIG (mortgage indemnity guarantee) fee, which can cost £1,000 or more.
● Whether the lender pays any upfront fees for you, such as solicitors' or surveyors' costs.

CHOOSING HOW YOU WILL REPAY YOUR MORTGAGE

It is not just the interest rate that you need to think about when deciding on your loan. Just as important is how you will repay it.

USING A REPAYMENT MORTGAGE

This is the simplest option. Each month you repay the interest on the loan and a proportion of the capital (the original amount you borrowed). It means that, whatever mortgage term you decide at the outset (often 25 years), you are guaranteed to have repaid the entire loan by that date. You will not see the outstanding balance fall by much in the first few years because most of your payments will be interest, but towards the end of the mortgage term almost all of your repayments will be capital.

PAYING OFF THE INTEREST ONLY

Here you just make interest payments throughout the life of the loan. At the end of the term, you will still have to pay off the original sum borrowed. Interest-only loans are normally set up alongside an investment plan, such as an ISA or an endowment policy, which is expected to mature at the end of the term with enough funds to pay off the original sum borrowed. Some people gamble on their property rising in value by enough to pay off the loan, but they still have to sell off the home at the end to pay off the loan.

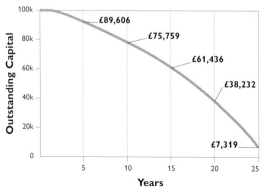

◀ **REDUCING CAPITAL**
With a repayment (or capital-and-interest) mortgage, you do pay off little more than interest in the early years. However, the balance will reduce sharply in later years, so that it is all paid off at the end of the term. This graph shows how much capital would be outstanding at the beginning of each year on a £100,000 repayment mortgage over 25 years.

UNDERSTANDING ENDOWMENTS

These products are plans that combine investment and life insurance. Endowments are designed to pay off your mortgage at the end of the term, or earlier in the event of your death. However, they have encountered a lot of criticism over recent years, mainly because the returns have fallen quite sharply and millions of people now face the prospect of their policies not making enough to pay off the debt. A number of lenders have stopped offering endowment mortgages altogether, and you should think seriously before you sign up to one. They are long-term contracts with high costs and charges and can be inflexible if your circumstances change.

DECIDING TO INVEST IN AN ISA

Like endowments, an individual savings account (ISA) can be used alongside an interest-only loan. You can invest cash, life insurance, or shares (usually in the form of a share-based fund such as a unit trust) in an ISA and returns are tax-free. There are annual limits on how much you can pay into one. As with endowments, there is no guarantee that your ISA will repay your loan in full at maturity. Unlike endowments, however, ISAs do not have built-in life insurance, but they can be cashed in at any time. If the stock market has fallen, you could get back less than you expect.

17 It is tempting to go for the easiest mortgage option, but it is a long-term contract so make sure it is the right one.

REPAYING USING A PRIVATE PENSION

You can use a private pension to repay your mortgage. However, this option is unsuitable for most people. Personal (and stakeholder) pensions allow you to take 25% of the fund as a tax-free lump sum at retirement. With a pension mortgage, you use this money to repay your loan. Pensions have generous tax relief, particularly for higher rate taxpayers. However, by taking part of your fund to repay your loan, you are reducing the amount available for retirement. You also have to tie in your mortgage redemption date with your retirement date, so if you start a pension mortgage early, you will pay interest for a long time.

LOOKING AT OTHER MORTGAGE CHOICES

T*here are other mortgage options, some of which may help people who might normally struggle to qualify for a loan, such as the self-employed and people with credit problems.*

OPTING FOR SELF-CERTIFICATION

If you have recently become self-employed, or if you have a very efficient accountant who ensures your accounts reflect the lowest income possible to avoid paying too much tax, you could have problems getting a loan through the normal procedure. Many lenders will take a more flexible approach if you are borrowing a small amount relative to the value of the property, but at levels above 75% of the purchase price, their criteria become much stricter. Using the self-certification method, you do not have to prove your income. The lender may contact your accountant to verify that you are self-employed and will normally check your credit file and carry out a credit score. Using this method, you should not have a pay a punitive rate of interest, but you will almost certainly find that you will not be able to get the most competitive deals. You will probably also find that most lenders will not normally let you borrow more than 85% of the purchase price, although there are exceptions to this so check with your financial adviser.

GETTING A NON-STATUS MORTGAGE

Non-status loans are aimed at people who have had credit problems such as a bankruptcy, people with no credit history, such as divorced women who have not had bills in their own name, or people who have income from an "unrecognized" source, such as maintenance payments. You will have to pay a higher rate of interest.

18 Some non-status loans are much more expensive than others, so shop around.

APPLYING FOR A GUARANTOR LOAN

Buyers who do not have a large enough income to borrow the amount they need can ask others (usually parents) to be guarantors. Guarantors have to make the repayments if the borrower fails to repay, so they must take legal advice.

CHOOSING A FLEXIBLE MORTGAGE

With a flexible mortgage, you apply for the loan in the same as you would an ordinary mortgage, but it means you can pay off the loan more quickly without penalties, or you can even use your mortgage as a reserve to call on when you need it. An increasing number of lenders are offering flexible mortgages, although the level of flexibility varies greatly from lender to lender. Many banks and building societies have branded some of their mortgages as "flexible" when their loans may have only one or two of the features of a flexible mortgage, so always carry out some comparisons before you decide. Truly flexible mortgages usually do the following:

- Allow you to make overpayments – either a regular monthly amount or a one-off payment.
- Let you take payment holidays once you have paid your loan for a certain time, or overpaid.
- Allow you to borrow back additional money you have paid.
- Charge interest daily (or weekly) so that your debt reduces more quickly. It also means that any additional money you pay is credited to your account straight away. Flexible mortgage rates can be slightly higher than traditional loans, so if you only want to pay off your mortgage as quickly as possible, you may not need all the features of a flexible loan.

USING AN OFFSET MORTGAGE FACILITY

Some flexible mortgages now offer an "offset" facility. Here the amount you owe is offset against any savings you may have with the lender and you only pay interest on the outstanding amount. It has the advantage of lowering your interest payments, but it does mean your savings, mortgage, and any personal loans are with the same bank or building society, which is unlikely to have the most competitive rates across the board.

19 You can use a flexible mortgage to overpay with money saved for large bills and draw it out again later.

EXERCISING CAUTION WITH FLEXIBLE LOANS

If you are not very disciplined about borrowing money, it would be best to avoid a mortgage that lets you borrow more easily. Research shows that many people with flexible mortgages pay more than the standard payments they are required to make, but if you take payment holidays or underpay on your loan, you could have problems in later years.

GETTING YOUR MORTGAGE

Once your offer has been accepted, and you have chosen the best mortgage, it is time to apply for the loan. This stage will be less stressful if you understand the process and are prepared.

MAKING THE APPLICATION

Your loan application is an important part of the information that a lender will rely on when deciding whether or not to grant you a mortgage. The longer it takes for you to be approved for a loan, the greater the chance for things to go wrong. This is particularly true if you are part of a chain, so do everything you can to help speed it up.

Cash

COUNTING YOUR CASH ▶

Mortgage lenders require home buyers to show they have enough cash to cover the deposit (assuming there is one) and whether it is their own money or a gift. They will not require proof that you can afford fees on top. You may need to provide the lender with the past three to six months' worth of bank statements, so it is worth making sure your account is in credit and that you have boosted your savings in the run-up to the application.

YOUR BANK		STATEMENT OF ACCOUNT			
Your Bank Card Services PO Box 001 Anytown QX00 1YZ	Name MS SUSAN THORLEY Account number 1234 5555 6789 1010			PAGE 1 OF 1 Statement date 6 APRIL	
Transaction date	Particulars		Withdrawn	Paid in	Balance
	BALANCE BROUGHT FORWARD				1000.00
28 FEB	BAC SALARY			2000.00	3000.00
25 MAR	0010 DORLING KINDERSLEY (BOOKSHOP)		8.99		2991.01
26 MAR	D/D WATER BOARD		12.99		2978.02
28 MAR	D/D CAR INSURANCE		45.50		2932.52
30 MAR	0011 THE GREEN PETROL STATION		25.50		2907.02
31 MAR	0012 HATS & COATS BOUTIQUE		75.94		2831.08
27 FEB	0009 PETROL PUMP		25.50		1000.00

▼ PROVING YOUR INCOME

You will need to prove your ability to repay what you borrow by providing the lender with payslips for the last three months, and your last P60. The lender may then contact your employer to check that the details you have given are correct. If you have only recently started your job, the attitude of the lender will depend on whether you have moved to another job within the same company, or if you have moved from a different employer entirely. If you are on a short-term contract, you still should be able to qualify for a loan from a mainstream lender, without paying penalty rates, as long as you can demonstrate that you have been on contract for a year, or that you have at least six months outstanding on a year-long contract.

THINGS TO KNOW

- If you know your salary is about to rise, you can apply for a mortgage on the new amount subject to final confirmation, which will save time later on.
- You will normally need to pay for the property valuation when you apply for the loan.
- The lender may charge an arrangement fee when you apply for the loan, or when you complete the purchase. You may be allowed to add the arrangement fee to the loan, but you will pay interest on it.

◄ CHECKING YOUR FILE

Lenders will be looking at how you handle debt, and you will need to prove you have been a trustworthy borrower in the past. Your credit file will provide them with at least the following information:

- *Whether you have repaid loans on time.*
- *The amount of debt you have applied for and how much you currently owe.*
- *Whether you have any County Court Judgments (CCJs) against your name.*
- *Whether you are on the electoral roll.*

Credit

Income

20 If you are self-employed, it does not matter how high your gross income is – the lender is only interested in your net income.

UNDERSTANDING THE MORTGAGE OFFER

*L*enders lay out all their terms in detailed legal language in
*the mortgage offer. When you, the borrower, agree to the
terms of the offer, you are promising to repay the loan. Several
areas are covered in the mortgage offer.*

LOAN AMOUNT

The amount you borrow is called the
advance. Usually, home buyers borrow
the difference between the deposit and
the selling price. If you cannot pay
upfront fees, they can be added to the
mortgage, but try to avoid this
because you will pay more in interest.

TYPE OF LOAN

The document will tell you whether you
have opted for a repayment loan (also
called capital and interest) or interest only.

THINGS TO KNOW

● Offer documents issued by lenders vary
  considerably. It is essential that you read
  the offer carefully and make sure you
  understand it because it forms the basis of
  your agreement with the lender. Most
  mortgage-offer documents have several
  pages of conditions, which set out the
  details of the loan. Once you have checked
  that the loan you are being offered is the
  one you applied for (for example a two-
  year discount rate with no penalties
  beyond the two years), you should study
  the other conditions carefully and, if
  necessary, ask for an explanation.

21 Mortgages can be set up incorrectly, so check the loan offer carefully.

CHARGING EXTRA FEES

You will be charged a fee for bounced cheques and for failed direct debits. Once you are in arrears, costs can mount up quickly.

REPAYMENT TERMS

Details of how and when you will repay the loan will be included in the mortgage offer.
Length of time. This indicates how long the mortgage will last. The typical length is 25 years for first-time buyers, although it can be shorter or longer. Check that the offer document contains the correct mortgage term.
Variability. The mortgage offer will give details of what rate you will pay, and whether it is fixed or variable. If it is variable, it will state the discount level. If it is a tracker, it will give the margin above the Bank of England base rate. It will also state how long the preferential rate will last.

INSURANCE DETAILS

The lender will require that you do not insure the property for less than the rebuilding cost specified in the property valuation. Some mortgage deals require you to take the lender's buildings and/or contents insurance. If yours does, the document will tell you. If you insure through the lender, it may add any unpaid insurance premiums on to the mortgage amount. If you arrange your insurance with another insurance company, or via a broker, you should tell the lender in writing which company you are using before exchange of contracts. Your solicitor should not exchange contracts until the lender has confirmed receipt of your notification.

STUDYING THE LOAN DOCUMENTATION

The lender will send you different documents about conditions relating to your loan. Read them carefully and keep them for future reference.

CONFIRMING ARRANGEMENTS

The lender will send you a document confirming details of the mortgage advance, including the term and the interest rate. It will also tell you how much your first monthly mortgage payment will be and when it will be deducted from your bank account. The first payment is often larger than subsequent ones, because it includes interest due in the month of completion as well as the normal monthly payment.

FAILING TO REPAY ON TIME

The lender will also supply information on what would happen, and what the likely costs would be, if you failed to repay your mortgage. You are normally charged an additional fee for every month your account is in arrears, once it is two months or more in arrears. You could also incur charges if you have to be visited by one of the lender's employees for recovery of debts, if the lender has to write to you about your arrears, if cheques bounce, or if direct debit payments are not made. Ultimately the lender has the right to repossess your property if you do not pay.

22 Review your documents carefully and ask questions if you are not happy.

ABIDING BY THE RULES

If you are using a mortgage broker or financial adviser, he or she is bound by a code of practice when giving you financial advice and has to abide by certain rules. If you are dealing with the lender direct, similar rules apply. Your broker or mortgage lender will tell you what these rules are. They will also tell you which of the three levels of service they are able to provide:

- Advice and a recommendation – the adviser will recommend a specific mortgage from their own range or from the entire market.
- Information – the adviser will tell you about several mortgages, but you make the choice about which one you want.
- Information on a single mortgage – where there is only one mortgage product on offer, or where you know exactly what you want.

23

Lenders may use call centres to handle mortgage processing. If you experience problems, get the name and direct dial number of the person you called.

DEALING WITH COMPLAINTS

Lenders and mortgage brokers are monitored independently to make sure that they are dealing with clients correctly and within current guidelines. However, that does not mean that you cannot make your own complaint. There are several recognized complaints schemes and your lender or broker should tell you which scheme they have joined.

UNDERSTANDING THE LEGAL CHARGE

Your mortgage is secured on the property you buy. This means that the lender (or mortgagee) who lends you the mortgage has a charge over the property; in other words, the company has the first call on the funds available when the property is sold. The mortgage deed is the document you sign to confirm that the lender has a legal charge and it will refer to the rights and obligations of both parties.

BUYING YOUR HOME

You have chosen a home, selected a mortgage, and been approved for a loan. Now you need to make some decisions that will affect the ongoing ownership of your home.

RECORDING OWNERSHIP

Each of the various ways you can own your property has legal and tax planning ramifications. Your solicitor or conveyancer will discuss the ownership with you and give you advice.

DEFINING TITLE

Title is the term for ownership, and the people whose names appear on the title deed are the only legal owners of the property. Once you have completed the purchase of the property, your name will appear on the title deed. The document is held by the mortgage lender until you have either paid off your loan at the end of the term, or remortgaged. If your property is leasehold, your interest will be recorded on the lease, and you will be given a copy. The lease will outline your responsibilities and duties as the leaseholder, and the responsibilities and duties of the freeholder.

HOLDING TITLE AS JOINT TENANTS

In joint tenancy, two or more people own an equal share in the property and it is the way that married couples typically own the family home. When one of the joint tenants dies, his or her share automatically goes to any surviving tenants no matter what is stated in the will. It does not become part of the estate to be divided between other beneficiaries, which means that property passing from one joint tenant to another does not go through probate proceedings. For the home to be sold, all joint tenants must agree to the sale.

OWNING PROPERTY AS TENANTS IN COMMON

If you are buying a house as an unmarried couple, or with a few friends, you are more likely to purchase as tenants in common. Here, instead of splitting ownership equally, it can be divided in any appropriate way. Each of you can own a share relating to the original percentage you paid towards the purchase price, for example. When a tenant in common dies, that person's share of the property forms part of his or her estate, to be passed on according to the will. The tenant in common has far more control over who benefits from his or her share of the property on death, but there could be tax implications.

BECOMING LIABLE FOR INHERITANCE TAX

Once you become a property owner, you may also unwittingly pick up a potential inheritance tax (IHT) liability along the way. Inheritance tax on your estate is payable by your heirs once your estate reaches a certain value. You can check the IHT threshold by asking your tax adviser. The threshold is regularly increased in the annual budget, so remember to check the current figure each year. With property prices in many parts of Britain having risen sharply for a number of years, more and more homeowners are incurring an IHT liability. Inheritance tax is paid by the people who benefit from your estate after your death and is charged at 40%. It does not automatically mean they will end up paying an IHT bill, since money and assets passed between husband and wife on death are exempt from IHT and steps can be taken to minimize liability by incorporating IHT planning when you draw up a will. It is particularly important for unmarried couples to get sound tax advice, because property passed between people who are not married attracts IHT.

HAVING SOLE OWNERSHIP

A sole owner owns 100% of the property in his or her name, which is the only name that appears on the title deed.

COHABITING COUPLES

If you are buying a property with your partner, it is important to draw up a will if you choose to own as tenants in common, otherwise your share of the property may not go to your partner on your death.

USING A SOLICITOR

Y*ou do not have to use a solicitor to help you through the homebuying process, but conveyancing matters can be complex so the do-it-yourself route may be best avoided.*

FINDING A SOLICITOR

As soon as you have put an offer in on a property and have had it accepted, the estate agent may suggest you instruct a solicitor local to the area who specializes in conveyancing. You do not have to use this solicitor and you should not feel under any pressure to do so. If you already have a solicitor, or can find one through recommendation, you will probably prefer to use that one instead. A licensed conveyancer, who is a specialist property lawyer, is also allowed to handle property transactions. If you do not have any personal recommendations, shop around to find a solicitor or conveyancer by obtaining a few quotes from different firms. Try to speak to the person who would be dealing with your purchase – it is important to feel comfortable with the solicitor you have chosen.

VERIFYING INFORMATION

Your solicitor (or conveyancer) will negotiate and agree the terms of the contract for the purchase. He or she will make sure the legal status of the property you plan to buy is suitable (for example that it is owned by the sellers and that there are no damaging issues relating to rights of way). Your solicitor will also clarify any information that the seller has provided (via the seller's solicitors) and keep you informed about what is found. Much of your solicitor's time leading up to exchange of contracts is spent trying to establish and verify relevant data. When your solicitor is happy, he or she will send a copy of the contract to you to be signed.

◀ **GETTING ALL THE FACTS**
Your solicitor should keep you in the picture about how the purchase is progressing, but there may be times when little new information is available.

COUNTING THE COST

The cost of conveyancing varies between solicitors and in different parts of the country. Typically, you could pay around £200 to £350 if the process is straightforward, but that cost could escalate if there are problems along the way. VAT will be charged on top of that, along with extras such as search fees.

KEEPING THE DEAL MOVING

Your solicitor will make sure that the process moves as smoothly as possible to exchange of contracts. Of course, this can be easier said than done, particularly if your transaction forms part of a chain and is dependent on other transactions progressing smoothly and on time. If the other parties' solicitors are raising queries about their contracts, there is little yours can do. Try to make sure that your solicitor keeps you informed, because it will reduce your stress levels. Do not make needless telephone calls but, if you feel you are being left in the dark, do not be afraid to telephone and ask questions. Increasingly, more solicitors are happy for their clients to communicate with them via e-mail, because they can reply to points you have raised as they deal with them, rather than specifically when you telephone. It also means you automatically receive the communication in a form that you can refer to later.

MAKING A COMPLAINT

If you are unhappy with the way your solicitor has handled the conveyancing, you should first address your complaint to your solicitor, or to someone else in the firm. If, however, the complaint concerns the solicitor's conduct, such as allegations of conflict of interest, or you are unhappy with the way the complaint has been handled, you should contact the regulatory body, the Office for the Supervision of Solicitors (OSS). There are strict time limits for complaints, especially if they concern fees.

24 Your solicitor will not send you a bill that you can pay later – it is all settled at completion.

UNDERSTANDING SURVEYS

*W*hen you apply for your mortgage, you will be charged for a valuation of your property to be carried out and you will also have to arrange your own survey. The mortgage valuation is purely for the benefit of the lender to make sure the property is a good security for the loan. There are several different types of survey, and the size and age of the property you are buying may help determine the right survey for you.

PAYING FOR A VALUATION

The valuation that the lender carries out on the property is is not strictly a survey, because it is designed principally to ensure that the property is worth the amount the buyer wants to borrow. It carries only basic information about the construction of the property and the current state of repair. However, in most cases, the cost of the valuation is passed on to the borrower. Most lenders charge for the valuation on a sliding scale, according to the price of the property, and some levy an administration charge on top, which will increase the cost. Check the administration charge and valuation fee before you apply for the mortgage. Some lenders will not charge borrowers for the cost of the valuation, but they will not let them see a copy of the report either. Others take a different view and provide more detailed information for borrowers in their valuations, such as an energy efficiency report, major structural defects, and the cost of repairs.

GETTING YOUR OWN SURVEY

There are two main types of survey: **Homebuyer's report and valuation.** This report was previously called a homebuyer's survey, and is designed to survey more modern houses (built in the 1960s onwards) and flats of conventional construction (for example, bricks and mortar). It should reveal serious defects, but may not specify how these should be remedied, or how significant they could be.

Building survey. This survey (formerly known as a structural survey) is the most detailed and therefore the most expensive. It can be used for most buildings and should reveal not only significant defects, but how these can be put right. Minor defects should be highlighted, along with the general maintenance of the building, and the standard of relevant fixtures and fittings.

Compare charges with several different surveyors because fees can vary widely.

THINGS TO KNOW

- Some valuation companies are owned by lenders, but this is not always disclosed to the buyer.
- Do not try to save money by using the same surveyor for the valuation and your own survey. You have different priorities for each one. You want the valuer to maximize the property's price and the surveyor to help you negotiate the price downwards, which is impossible for the same person to do.

ARRANGING OTHER INSPECTIONS

Your surveyor may recommend that you follow up concerns that have been raised in the survey by having a detailed investigation for damp, or that appliances such as central heating boilers are tested by a CORGI-registered engineer, and that wiring is tested by an NICEIC-registered electrician. You may be tempted to save money at this stage, but bear in mind that it could cost you much more than the price of the investigations if there is a serious problem.

SAVING YOURSELF MONEY

It is always advisable to have your own survey carried out on a property. Never rely on the lender's valuation alone. A detailed report will identify any potential problems before you commit yourself to buying a property, which can save you a lot of money later. It will also give you a chance to renegotiate the sale price with the seller. If the survey helps you get the price reduced by a few hundred or a few thousand pounds, this in itself will more than make up for the surveyor's fee.

AVOIDING UNEXPECTED BILLS

All chartered surveyors carry their own professional indemnity insurance in the event of a claim against them for failing to spot a problem that should have been apparent. However, in cases where the surveyor could not examine the relevant part of the building, you will not have a claim. You can avoid this problem by taking out "hidden defects" insurance, which covers buyers who have had a homebuyer's report or building survey. It does not cover all problems, but it will pay out for very serious defects. Some lenders provide it free with the survey, otherwise it is possible to buy it as a stand-alone policy.

ADDING UP THE COSTS

*B*e sure you are prepared for the many expenses involved in buying a home. Many buyers have to pay stamp duty of at least 1% of the purchase price. With legal and survey fees, the extras could add up to several thousand pounds.

ESTIMATING APPLICATION COSTS

The lender's fees will probably include the following:

Arrangement fee. This is typically a few hundred pounds and is non-refundable. Not all mortgages will involve an arrangement fee, but typically some of the preferential rates will. A booking fee is normally charged on fixed rate mortgages, where the money for the loan has to be purchased in advance on the money markets.

Mortgage valuation fee. Some lenders require you to enclose payment for the property valuation fee when you apply for the mortgage. The fee varies according to the price of the property.

25 Mortgage fees and other costs can tip the balance between two otherwise identical loan rates.

INCLUDING COSTS THAT PROTECT YOU

Your solicitor should give you an idea of what the disbursements, such as the costs of various searches, could be. Many of these protect your interests.

Land Registry search fee. This search makes sure that the sellers own the property and that there are no unknown debts registered against it.

Local search fee. This search is conducted by the local authority to release information about whether any planning applications have been made for work near your property, such as road or rail proposals.

Draining search fee. This establishes the status of the drainage system and will tell you whether the property has a water meter fitted.

TAKING STAMP DUTY INTO ACCOUNT

One of the biggest bills, which many first-time buyers forget to take into account, is stamp duty. This is one of those charges that no one wants to pay – especially now that it can account for a bill of up to 4% of the property price. Stamp duty was introduced some 300 years ago and is charged for the actual "stamping" of documents that happens when property is transferred from one owner to another. Rates vary, so check the current levels with your solicitor. The difference in cost between a property that is in a lower stamp-duty band and one that is only slightly more expensive, but in a higher band, can be significant. It is worth bearing in mind when you are negotiating on price.

ALLOWING FOR OTHER COSTS

There will be other costs that you will have to pay before you can finally live in your new home. These include:

Telegraphic transfer fee. The quickest and most secure way to transfer money on completion day is via telegraphic transfer. The bank will charge an additional fee for this service, so check the current fee with your solicitor.

Mortgage broker. Your mortgage broker may charge you a fee for finding your mortgage and dealing with the application. This may be a fixed amount or a percentage of the value of the loan (normally up to 1%).

ANTICIPATING LEASEHOLD COSTS

If you are buying a leasehold property, you will normally have to pay a percentage of the service charge relating to the year in which you are buying. Depending on the annual service charge level and when you buy the property, this could amount to several hundred pounds, and much more if the building is expensive to run, for example if you need to maintain a lift in the building or a swimming pool or gym, or you have to contribute towards the cost of a porter.

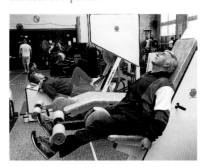

**PAYING FOR ▶
EXTRA FACILITIES**
If there are additional facilities in your building, such as a gym or a swimming pool, as a leaseholder you will be expected to contribute towards the cost of maintaining it.

ARRANGING INSURANCE

*B*efore buying a home, make sure you add in the cost of insurance. How much and what types of insurance you need are important decisions to ensure that you protect your home's structure and any valuables.

PROTECTING THE STRUCTURE

Buildings insurance is designed to cover the cost of repairing or rebuilding your property if it is damaged by something like fire, flood, vandalism, or subsidence. When you are shopping around for insurance, companies will want to know when the property was built, how many bedrooms it has, and what type of construction it is. They will also ask for information relating to the rebuilding value, which is not the selling price or its market value, but an estimate of the actual cost of rebuilding your property. Most surveyors include this in the valuation, homebuyer's report, or building survey. Check that yours will before the survey.

DECIDING ON THE LEVEL OF COVER REQUIRED

Policies differ between insurers in terms of what they cover. Check to see if you are covered for:
- Garden furniture and plants.
- Reimbursement of hotel costs if you cannot remain in your property.
- "Seek and find", which pays the cost of finding a problem's cause, so if there is a leak in your kitchen, you can claim not only the cost of any damage but also money spent locating the leak.

GETTING THE RIGHT AMOUNT OF COVER

If your surveyor does not provide an estimate of rebuilding costs, you can get a rough estimate of what it will be if you know the size of your home. The Association of British Insurers, which represents most insurers operating in the UK, has a rebuilding cost calculator on its website (log on to www.abi.org.uk). Type in the external area in square metres or square feet, the type of property, and when it was built. The calculator will then ask you for the location of the property in the UK, and whether there is a garage or outbuildings.

INSURING FOR PERSONAL INJURIES

Taking out liability insurance protects you in the event you are sued by someone injured on your property. People may try to sue you whether they were invited or uninvited guests.

TAKING OUT CONTENTS INSURANCE

As well as insuring the building, you will want to make sure your belongings are covered. Most policies insure on a "new-for-old" basis, which means you will get your possessions replaced with new ones, whatever their age when you claim. The amount you insure for is usually based on the number of bedrooms and whether you are buying a house or a flat. There are useful extras that you can add to your policy:

- Accidental damage, either for specific items or all contents. If you are on a tight budget, shop around for quotes with and without this benefit.
- Personal possessions, which covers valuable items (such as jewellery) both while they are in the home and when you take them elsewhere.

REDUCING THE COST

When you start shopping around for insurance, you are likely to find wide variations in the quotes of different companies. You may be able to reduce the cost by:

- Looking at the discounts offered by various companies. Some may lower the premium if you buy several policies (such as buildings, contents, and motor insurance) from them.
- Fitting approved window locks, an approved burglar alarm, or becoming a member of your local Neighbourhood Watch scheme.
- Raising the excess levels on your insurance policies. However, be careful not to increase them to a level that you could not afford.

USING LEASEHOLD BLOCK INSURANCE

If you live in a leasehold flat, the buildings insurance is normally arranged by the landlord, or the landlord's managing agent, and paid for annually as part of the service charge. Your landlord may also charge a commission on top. If the leaseholders manage the block, or own the freehold between them, they may sort out the insurance directly themselves or they may use a managing agent to arrange the insurance cover on their behalf.

INSURING YOUR MORTGAGE

When you arrange your mortgage, there are several insurance options you need to consider. They may not all be appropriate to you, and can be expensive. Your financial adviser should help you decide your priorities.

TAKING OUT LIFE INSURANCE

If you are married, own the property with a partner or friends, or have children or other dependants, you will need life insurance to ensure that the mortgage is paid off in the event of your death. If you have an endowment mortgage, it is already included in the policy. Most joint mortgages are covered by a policy that will pay out on the first death, no matter which person dies first.

LOOKING AT LIFE INSURANCE OPTIONS

There are different life insurance policies available:

Whole-of-life policy. This will pay out a predetermined sum whenever you die, whether it is during the mortgage term or afterwards.

Term insurance. This will pay out only if you die within the mortgage term. There are two types of term insurance: level or decreasing. With level term insurance, the amount of cover remains constant, which makes it most suitable for people who have interest-only mortgages. Decreasing term insurance provides cover that falls in line with your capital repayments, so it is appropriate for people with a repayment mortgage. It is cheaper than level term insurance, although the premiums remain the same throughout the policy's life.

26 Premiums for life insurance are based on your age, sex, and health. Shop around because rates can vary widely.

27 People who took out a mortgage after 1 October 1995 cannot claim state mortgage support for the first nine months of their claim.

PROTECTING YOUR MORTGAGE

This policy is also known as accident, sickness, and unemployment insurance and is normally offered at the time you arrange your mortgage. It is designed to pay your monthly mortgage premiums if you cannot work due to illness or redundancy. Payments normally stop after a limited time – often 12 or 24 months – and do not come into effect until 30 or more days after the first date of the claim. If you are self-employed, you may find it hard to make a claim under the redundancy section of your policy unless your business has failed. Similarly, people on short-term contracts may not be eligible to take out a policy in the first place. If it is appropriate for you, it is much cheaper to buy when you take out your mortgage than at a later date.

GETTING CRITICAL ILLNESS INSURANCE

This insurance pays out a tax-free lump sum if you are diagnosed with one of a specified list of serious illnesses, including cancer, stroke, and heart disease. The policy can last either for the mortgage term only, or for longer. In general terms, the more diseases that are covered in your policy, the more expensive it is. If you have a repayment mortgage, the size of the lump sum you insure for usually falls in line with the outstanding amount owed.

THINGS TO KNOW

● The list of conditions covered by critical illness insurance varies between different insurance providers. With some illnesses, you may not get a payout on diagnosis, but when the condition is deemed sufficiently serious.

● When you apply for critical illness insurance, you will be required to provide details of your medical history and will normally have to have a medical examination. Existing medical conditions will not be covered, including any pre-existing conditions not disclosed at the time of making the application for insurance cover.

APPROACHING EXCHANGE AND COMPLETION

You do not have to know all the legalities involved in buying a home, but if you have a basic understanding about what should happen at the key stages you will feel more in control.

GATHERING INFORMATION

When you instruct your solicitor or conveyancer to act on your behalf, the initial steps he or she takes are designed to find out as much relevant information about the property as possible. A range of searches will have been carried out, from local authority searches to drainage and environmental information (designed primarily to comply with regulations governing contaminated land). Your sellers will have been asked to complete a form with a list of detailed questions, including who is responsible for boundary walls, which items they propose leaving at the property, and which items they will be taking with them. Some of the answers may be ambiguous, or the seller may not know, and your solicitor will have followed these up and then made further enquiries.

MAKING FINAL PREPARATIONS

Your solicitor will get all the points clarified before he or she is prepared to proceed towards exchange of contracts. At this point your solicitor will send you a written report explaining what has been done, and a copy of the contract will be enclosed for signing. Unless it is coming from the proceeds of a sale, you will have to send the deposit, which can be 5% or 10% of the purchase price. Most people use a same-day electronic payment system called CHAPS.

EXCHANGING CONTRACTS

Once the contracts have been signed, exchange can take place. However, if you are in a chain, it will not take place until the slowest party is ready. Signed contracts can remain on file for several weeks before exchange, which is just a telephone call between solicitors followed by the contracts in the post. As soon as the solicitors exchange contracts by telephone the sale is binding, and you could incur heavy costs if you back out.

PREPARING FOR COMPLETION

The period between exchange of contracts to completion is generally between 2 and 4 weeks, and during this time your solicitor will submit a certificate of title to the mortgage lender and will request that the advance is available on a specified day. A document will be prepared, which will be signed by the sellers before going to the Inland Revenue to be stamped for stamp duty. Another Land Registry search is done to make sure nothing has changed between the first one and completion, and a bankruptcy search is carried out on behalf of the mortgage lender. A financial statement will also be prepared, which will show you how much you have to pay at completion.

ARRANGING INSURANCE

Your buildings insurance should take effect from exchange of contracts, so make sure it is set up in time. However, your contents policy does not need to provide cover until the completion date. Check whether your possessions will be covered in the move if you do not use a professional removal firm. You will also need to inform your car insurers that you are moving to a new address, and you may possibly pay more (or less) for your cover.

COMPLETING THE PURCHASE

Completion takes place when the outstanding money is paid to the seller. The estate agent should give you a provisional completion time, but he or she will check that money has been successfully transferred to the seller before handing over the keys.

TIMING YOUR MOVE

Many people move on the last Friday of the month, because interest is charged from completion, but the first payment is not taken until the month following completion. In this way, the first mortgage payment is kept as low as possible. However, banks are often slower at transferring money because of the volume of completions, and occasionally payments can get held up.

ARRANGING YOUR MOVE

The day you move into your new home is bound to be an exciting one. However, it can also be stressful. Do your research and planning in advance to help it all go smoothly.

ORGANIZING REMOVALS

In the weeks before your move you will have plenty to keep you occupied, but it is important to find time to organize how you will move your possessions to your new home.

- Telephone at least three removal companies (unless you plan to do it yourself). Removal quotes can vary widely, so it is worth shopping around. The cost will depend on the size of the property, where you live, and whether you plan on doing some or all of the packing yourself or getting the firm to do all the hard work.
- You will not be able to book the firm until you know your completion date. Bear in mind that most will be much busier on the last Friday of the month and you may need to book them at least ten days in advance.

DEALING WITH UTILITIES

Taking over gas, electricity, and water supplies should be straightforward. With gas and electricity, you should arrange to take a final meter reading when you leave your old property, and another when you move into your new home. You may want to use the move as an opportunity to shop around for cheaper gas and electricity. Energywatch, the energy watchdog, has a facility on its website (log on to www.energywatch.org.uk) that you can use to compare tariffs between different companies. Contact your water supplier and, if you have a meter, take a reading on the last day as with gas and electricity. Otherwise simply inform them of your moving date and new address.

28 Getting the removal firm to do the packing does not cost much more than doing it yourself – the firm's insurance then covers all breakages too.

THINGS TO KNOW

- If you are moving into an area that has the same STD code, you should be able to move your telephone number without paying anything extra. The telephone company will normally assume you take over the new telephone bill at midday on your moving day. As with gas and electricity, you may find that another provider can save you money. Log on to www.phonebills.org.uk and type in details of your current use and provider to find other telephone service providers in your area.
- To get your mail redirected to your new address, you can pick up a form at your local Post Office. You will be charged for each different surname, not for each address.

INFORMING COMPANIES OF YOUR NEW ADDRESS

You will have to contact a whole range of other companies to let them know your new address. Working your way through this list will help you to get started:

- Banks, building societies, credit card issuers, and pension/investment companies.
- Your employer, local tax office, and other Government departments such as the Benefits Agency, or Customs and Excise if you are registered for VAT.
- Insurance companies (for example car, travel, and life insurance).
- Local authority, to change council tax and electoral roll details.
- DVLC – to change a driving licence, get a form from the Post Office or DVLC website.

GETTING THE KEYS

You can now move in and enjoy your new home. Congratulations!

BUYING IN SCOTLAND AND NORTHERN IRELAND

The Scottish system of home-buying is quite different from the system south of the border. The biggest difference is that buyers in Scotland have a survey carried out at an earlier stage, before they have made an offer, and the whole process from offer to move is much quicker. In Northern Ireland the system is very similar to that in England and Wales.

BEGINNING YOUR SEARCH

Unlike in England and Wales, you cannot buy a home in Scotland without using a solicitor, and he or she generally gets involved in the process much earlier. In many areas, particularly larger cities, they have set up SSPCs – Scottish Solicitors' Property Centres – where they act as both the estate agent and solicitor. Traditional estate agents are still used by many buyers, although in some areas SSPCs have become more popular. In Northern Ireland, as in England and Wales, you can buy a home without using a solicitor.

NOTING INTEREST

In Scotland, when you find a property you like, you need to ask your solicitor to note your interest. It does not mean that you are obliged to proceed further, but it will enable the selling agent to be aware of your interest and keep you informed. You should get the property surveyed at this point.

ARRANGING A MORTGAGE

In Scotland, your solicitor will normally advise you to organize your mortgage before you start looking for property and certainly before you make an offer. That means applying for a "mortgage in principle" so that the loan is only dependent on a final credit check and valuation of the property. If your solicitor is regulated to give investment advice, he or she could arrange your mortgage as well, otherwise you should consult an independent mortgage adviser.

In Northern Ireland you do not have to arrange your mortgage in advance, but it will add to your credibility with sellers if you do so. There are fewer lenders available in Northern Ireland, however, so your choice may be limited.

---

 29 Gazumping does happen in Scotland, but it is rare.

MAKING THE OFFER

In Scotland, there are two types of property offer, known as "conditional" and "unconditional". Conditional offers are dependent on the results of a survey, whereas with an unconditional offer, the buyer would have had a survey carried out before he or she put in the offer. Most sellers will not be keen to accept a conditional offer, unless their property has been on the market for some time. If you put in an unconditional offer, it still gives your solicitor the right to raise any queries necessary and enter into negotiations. In Northern Ireland, the procedure is the same as the system in force in England and Wales.

 30 Scottish solicitors cannot act for a seller who wants to accept a higher offer after closing.

SETTING A CLOSING DATE

If several people are interested in the same property, it is usual in Scotland for the estate agent or solicitor to set a closing date. It means that anyone who is interested in buying must make a sealed offer at a specified time and date to the selling agent.

 31 The quicker a deal is finalized, the less time there is for something to go wrong.

PROCESSING THE TRANSACTION

The system in Northern Ireland is largely the same as that in force in England and Wales. In Scotland, however, the procedure is as follows:

Accepting the offer. If your offer is accepted, your solicitor will be informed in writing. It is normally "qualified", which means it may be followed by further negotiations.

Concluding the Missives. Until all the points have been dealt with, the contract (called *the Missives*) has not been concluded. Your solicitor and the seller's solicitor will try to deal with all the conditions attached to the offer – a process that normally takes between two and four weeks. Only when you are happy should you conclude because, once the Missives are concluded, you cannot renegotiate on any of the conditions.

Taking entry. This is the completion of the process. The purchase price is paid to the seller's solicitors on the date of settlement. Once there is confirmation that the money has been received, you can go to collect the keys and move into your new home.

LOOKING AHEAD

*O*nce you have moved, the last thing you will probably want to think *about is selling up, or switching your mortgage, but changes to your circumstances could make remortgaging worth considering. Planned reforms to the selling process could also affect you when you come to sell.*

WATCHING THE MORTGAGE MARKET

It is always worth keeping an eye on the mortgage market, because you could save yourself money by switching lenders. Before deciding, however, you should consider:

- Why you want to remortgage.
- The interest rate of your mortgage.
- The interest rate of a new mortgage.
- The cost of remortgaging.
- How much equity you have built up in your home.
- Your current income and the quality of your credit record.

You may want to remortgage to:

Pay a lower interest rate. You may find that you are able to get a new loan at a lower rate of interest, reducing your monthly payments. If you plan to remain in your home for several years, the savings could justify the costs of remortgaging.

Build equity faster. If you have a repayment mortgage, by remortgaging to a flexible lender you can overpay on your loan and increase the amount of equity in your home.

Switch from a variable to a fixed rate loan. Variable rate mortgages often offer lower interest rates than fixed rate loans, because you are taking a risk on interest rate levels. If you know you will be on a tight budget, a fixed rate will give you stable monthly payments.

Switch from a fixed to a variable rate loan. A variable rate loan, such as a discount or tracker, may lower your repayments. Remember, however, that your mortgage rate will rise as Bank of England rates increase. If your income has increased and you can accommodate a future rise in mortgage rates, it may be worth considering – but it is a risk.

Tap into your equity. If your property has risen in value, you may want to increase your mortgage, perhaps to pay for expenses such as home improvements. Take advice first though, because you will be increasing your debt. Try not to use it to pay off other bills.

RECEIVING INFORMATION ▶
You may feel a little like this, considering all the information available. However, staying informed can make investing in a home a financially rewarding experience.

KEEPING INFORMED

Pay attention to local and national news in order to keep in touch with the mortgage market. The internet is also a valuable source of information on mortgages and new homes.

CALCULATING REMORTGAGE COSTS

Before you think about remortgaging, find out if you would have to pay any redemption penalties. If so, ask your lender or broker to tell you how much they will cost in pounds (many are expressed as a percentage of the loan), then estimate your remortgaging costs. You will also need to allow several hundred pounds for survey and legal fees, unless you can find a deal that pays them for you. However, it may still be worth doing. A broker should be able to tell you how long it would take to offset your expenses.

UNDERSTANDING SELLER'S PACKS

In England and Wales, around 30% of transactions fail between the offer being accepted and contracts being exchanged, costing hundreds of millions of pounds. As a result, some experts believe that "seller's packs" can help to reduce the number of transactions that fail due to protracted delays before deals are finalized. Seller's packs simply give buyers certain information from the sellers in advance – including copies of the title deeds and search results. Also included in the pack is a condition report (a kind of survey), which sellers have to commission and pay for themselves. The main criticisms of these packs is that they cost several hundred pounds and have to be paid for in advance. There is also concern that buyers may not trust the seller's survey.

INDEX

ACKNOWLEDGMENTS

AUTHORS' ACKNOWLEDGMENTS

Sarah Pennells is very grateful to the people who assisted with this book, in particular Tyrone Silcott, a mortgage broker with independent financial advisers Everett Macleod, Simon Agace of Winkworth estate agents, for helping with facts and figures and checking details, and Andrew Flint, a conveyancing partner with solicitors Colman Coyle. Sarah would also like to thank Caroline Marklew of Portal Publishing and, most importantly, Lorraine Turner, for her invaluable expertise and guidance. Thanks also to Adèle Hayward, Sarah Cowley, Richard Gilbert, and Marianne Markham at Dorling Kindersley, who have been both professional and positive throughout.

Marc Robinson wishes to thank Joe Breckner, who gave his time, knowledge, experience, and enthusiasm to the project. Marc would like to dedicate this book to Zachary Robinson, and to Bert and Phoebe Robinson for all their patience and support.

PUBLISHER'S ACKNOWLEDGMENTS

Dorling Kindersley would like to thank everyone who generously lent props for the photo shoots, and the following for their help and participation:

Editorial Ruth Strother; Stephanie Rubenstein; **Design and Layout** Hedayat Sandjari; **Consultants** Nick Clemente; Skeeter; **Indexer** Caroline Curtis; **Proofreader** Fiona Biggs; **Photography** Anthony Nex; **Photographers' assistant** Damon Dumas; **Models** Joe Breckner; Ben Davis; Amanda Davis; **Picture researcher** Mark Dennis; Sam Ruston. **Special thanks to** Teresa Clavasquin for her generous support and assistance.

AUTHORS' BIOGRAPHIES

Sarah Pennells is a personal finance journalist who writes for a variety of magazines and newspapers and reports on BBC1's *Breakfast* programme and *It's Your Money* for BBC1 and News 24. Sarah regularly writes for the *Financial Mail on Sunday* and *Shares* magazine and is the personal finance editor for *The Lady*. She has also written for the London *Evening Standard* Homes and Property supplement and *Woman and Home* magazine.

Marc Robinson is a Founding Director of LEAP (Latino Education Achievement Project). He is also co-founder of Internet-based moneytours.com, a personal finance resource for corporations and other institutions. He wrote the original *The Wall Street Journal Guide to Understanding Money and Markets*, created *The Wall Street Journal Guide to Understanding Personal Finance*, and co-published a personal finance series with Time Life Books. He is also the author of the KISS guide on Personal Finance. In his two decades in the financial services industry, he has provided marketing consulting to many top Wall Street firms. He is admitted to practise law in New York State.

PICTURE CREDITS

Key: *a* above, *b* bottom, *c* centre, *l* left, *r* right, *t* top
The Image Bank/Getty Images: Don Klumpp 4c; **Washington Dolls' Museum:** German doll's house 55.